Tucholsky Wagner Zola Scott Sydow Freud Schlegel
Turgenev Wallace Fonatne Twain Walther von der Vogelweide Fouqué Friedrich II. von Preußen
Weber Freiligrath Frey
Fechner Fichte Weiße Rose von Fallersleben Kant Ernst Frommel
Richthofen
Hölderlin
Engels Fielding Eichendorff Tacitus Dumas
Fehrs Faber Flaubert
Feuerbach Maximilian I. von Habsburg Fock Eliasberg Zweig Ebner Eschenbach
Ewald Eliot Vergil
Goethe Elisabeth von Österreich London
Mendelssohn Balzac Shakespeare Dostojewski Ganghofer
Trackl Stevenson Lichtenberg Rathenau Doyle Gjellerup
Mommsen Tolstoi Hambruch Droste-Hülshoff
Thoma Lenz Hanrieder
von Arnim Hägele Humboldt
Dach Verne Hauff
Reuter Rousseau Hagen Hauptmann Gautier
Karrillon Garschin Baudelaire
Defoe Hebbel
Damaschke Descartes Hegel Kussmaul Herder
Wolfram von Eschenbach Dickens Schopenhauer Rilke George
Bronner Darwin Melville Grimm Jerome
Campe Horváth Aristoteles Bebel Proust
Bismarck Vigny Voltaire Federer Herodot
Gengenbach Barlach Heine
Storm Casanova Tersteegen Grillparzer Georgy
Chamberlain Lessing Langbein Gilm Gryphius
Brentano Lafontaine
Strachwitz Claudius Schiller Kralik Iffland Sokrates
Katharina II. von Rußland Bellamy Schilling
Gerstäcker Raabe Gibbon Tschechow
Löns Hesse Hoffmann Gogol Wilde Vulpius
Luther Heym Hofmannsthal Gleim
Roth Klee Hölty Morgenstern Goedicke
Heyse Klopstock Kleist
Luxemburg Puschkin Homer Mörike
La Roche Horaz Musil
Machiavelli
Navarra Aurel Musset Kierkegaard Kraft Kraus
Nestroy Marie de France Lamprecht Kind Kirchhoff Hugo Moltke
Laotse Ipsen Liebknecht
Nietzsche Nansen Ringelnatz
Marx Lassalle Gorki Klett
von Ossietzky May Leibniz
vom Stein Lawrence Irving
Petalozzi Knigge
Platon Pückler Michelangelo Kafka
Sachs Poe Kock
Liebermann Korolenko
de Sade Praetorius Mistral Zetkin

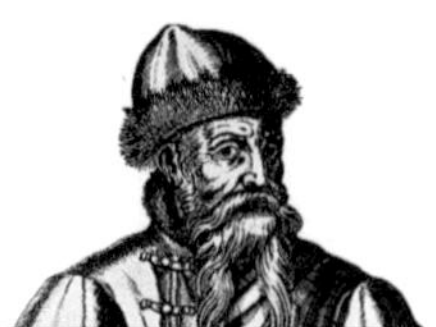

The publishing house tredition has created the series **TREDITION CLASSICS**. It contains classical literature works from over two thousand years. Most of these titles have been out of print and off the bookstore shelves for decades.

The book series is intended to preserve the cultural legacy and to promote the timeless works of classical literature. As a reader of a **TREDITION CLASSICS** book, the reader supports the mission to save many of the amazing works of world literature from oblivion.

The symbol of **TREDITION CLASSICS** is Johannes Gutenberg (1400 – 1468), the inventor of movable type printing.

With the series, tredition intends to make thousands of international literature classics available in printed format again – worldwide.

All books are available at book retailers worldwide in paperback and in hardcover. For more information please visit: www.tredition.com

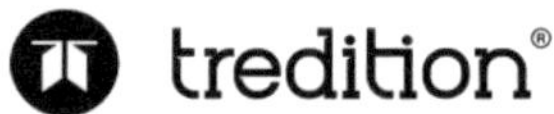

tredition was established in 2006 by Sandra Latusseck and Soenke Schulz. Based in Hamburg, Germany, tredition offers publishing solutions to authors and publishing houses, combined with worldwide distribution of printed and digital book content. tredition is uniquely positioned to enable authors and publishing houses to create books on their own terms and without conventional manufacturing risks.

For more information please visit: www.tredition.com

Sculpture of the Exposition Palaces and Courts

Juliet Helena Lumbard James

Imprint

This book is part of the TREDITION CLASSICS series.

Author: Juliet Helena Lumbard James
Cover design: toepferschumann, Berlin (Germany)

Publisher: tredition GmbH, Hamburg (Germany)
ISBN: 978-3-8491-4723-5

www.tredition.com
www.tredition.de

Sculpture of the Exposition Palaces and Courts

Descriptive Notes on the
Art of the Statuary at the
Panama-Pacific International Exposition
San Francisco

By

Juliet James

To A. Stirling Calder who has so ably managed the execution of
the sculpture, and to the vast body of sculptors and their workmen
who have given the world such inspiration with their splendid
work, this book is dedicated.

Foreword

What accents itself in the mind of the layman who makes even a cursory study of the sculptors and their works at the Panama-Pacific International Exposition is the fine, inspiring sincerity and uplift that each man brings to his work. One cannot be a great sculptor otherwise.

The sculptor's work calls for steadfastness of purpose through long years of study, acute observation, the highest standards, fine intellectual ability and above all a decided universalism - otherwise the world soon passes him by.

It is astonishing to see brought together the work of so many really great sculptors. America has a very large number of talented men expressing themselves on the plastic side - and a few geniuses.

The Exposition of 1915 has given the world the opportunity of seeing the purposeful heights to which these men have climbed.

We have today real American sculpture - work that savors of American soil - a splendid national expression.

Never before have so many remarkable works been brought together; and American sculpture is only in its infancy - born, one might say, after the Centennial Exposition of 1876.

The wholesome part of it all is that men and women are working independently in their expressions. We do not see that effect here of one man trying to fit himself to another man's clothing. The work is all distinctly individual. This individualism for any art is a hopeful outlook.

The sculpture has vitalized the whole marvelous Exposition. It is not an accessory, as has been the sculpture of previous Expositions, but it goes hand in hand with the architecture, poignantly existing for its own sake and adding greatly to the decorative architectural effects. In many cases the architecture is only the background or often only a pedestal for the figure or group, pregnant with spirit and meaning.

Those who have the city's growth at heart should see to it that these men of brain and skill and inspiration are employed to help beautify the commercial centers, the parks, the boulevards of our cities.

We need the fine lessons of beauty and uplift around us.

We beautify our houses and spend very little time in them. Why not beautify our outside world where we spend the bulk of our time?

We, a pleasure-loving people, are devoting more time every year to outside life. Would it not be a thorough joy to the most prosaic of us to have our cities beautified with inspiring sculpture?

We do a great deal in the line of horticultural beautifying - we could do far more - but how little we have done with one of the most meaningful and stimulating of the arts.

Let us see to it, in San Francisco at least, that a few of these works are made permanent.

Take as an example James Earle Fraser's "End of the Trail." Imagine the effect of that fine work silhouetted against the sky out near Fort Point, on a western headland, with the animal's head toward the sea, so that it would be evident to the onlooker that the Indian had reached the very end of the trail. It would play a wonderful part in the beauty of the landscape.

Or take Edith Woodman Burroughs' "Youth." What a delight a permanent reproduction of that fountain would be if placed against the side of one of the green hills out at Golden Gate Park - say near the Children's Playground - with a pool at its base. It is only by concerted action that we will ever get these works among us. Who is going to take the lead?

The Contents

The Signs of the Zodiac - Herman A. MacNeil, Sculptor
The Fountain of Ceres - Evelyn Beatrice Longman, Sculptor
The Survival of the Fittest - Robert Ingersoll Aitken, Sculptor
Earth - Robert Ingersoll Aitken, Sculptor
Wildflower - Edward Berge, Sculptor

Sculpture of the Exposition Palaces and Courts

"The influence of sculpture is far reaching. The mind that loves this art and understands its language will more and more insist on a certain order and decorum in visual life. It opens an avenue for the expression of aesthetic enjoyment somewhere between poetry and music and akin to drama. - Arthur Hoeber

The Fountain of Energy

A. Stirling Calder, Sculptor [See Frontispiece]

The Fountain of Energy is a monumental aquatic composition expressing in exuberant allegory the triumph of Energy, the Lord of the Isthmian Way. It is the central sculptural feature of the South Garden, occupying the great quatrefoil pool in front of the tower. The theme is Energy, the Conqueror - the Over Lord - the Master; Energy, mental and physical; Energy - the Will, the indomitable power that achieved the Waterway between the Oceans at Panama. The Earth Sphere, supported by an undulating frieze of mer-men and women, is his pedestal. Advancing from it in the water at the four relatively respective points of the compass, North, South, East and West, are groups representing the Atlantic and the Pacific Oceans and the North and the South Seas; groups richly imaginative, expressing types of Oriental, Occidental, Southern and Northern land and sea life. The interrupted outer circle of water motifs represent Nereids driving spouting fish. Vertical zones of writhing figures ascend the sphere at the base of the Victor. Across the upper portions of the sphere, and modeled as parts of the Earth, stretch titanic zoomorphs, representing the Hemispheres, East and West.

The spirit of the Eastern Hemisphere is conceived as feline and characterized as a human tiger cat. The spirit of the Western Hemisphere is conceived as taurine and characterized as a human bull. The base of the Equestrian is surrounded by a frieze of architecturalized fish and the rearing sea horses that furnish the principal upper motif for the play of water. Energy himself is presented as a nude male, typically American, standing in his stirrups astride a snorting charger - an exultant super-horse needing no rein - commanding with grandly elemental gesture of extended arms, the passage of the Canal. Growing from his shoulders, winged figures of Fame and Valor with trumpet, sword and laurel, forming a crest above his controlling head, acclaim his triumph. The Fountain embodies the mood of joyous, exultant power and exactly expresses the spirit of the Exposition. Its unique decorative character has been aptly described as heraldic, "The Power of America rising from the Sea."

A. Stirling Calder

The Mother of Tomorrow

A. Stirling Calder, Sculptor

With upturned face, with steady onward gaze, the stalwart Mother of Tomorrow moves ahead. Hers is the firm, determined purpose, the will to do - to accomplish that for which she has started. She marches ahead of the types of the Occident. It has taken all these types striving with common purpose to produce the future, therefore they form the Mother of Tomorrow, the matrix from which the future generations are to come. Mr. Calder's high, splendid ideals are directly mirrored in this one figure. It is not hard to read the man in his handiwork.

The Nations of the Occident

A. Stirling Calder, Frederick Roth, Leo Lentelli, Sculptors

Into the great Court of the Universe, from the top of the Arch of the
Occident, march the types of men who have made the Western civi-
lization.
 From left to right - the French-Canadian, the Alaskan, the German,
the
Latin-American, the Italian, the Anglo-American, the Squaw, the
American
Indian. In the center of this well-balanced pyramidal group, sur-
mounted
by Enterprise and drawn by sturdy oxen, comes the old prairie
schooner.
To right and left atop are seen the Heroes of Tomorrow - one a
white
boy, the other a negro type. In front marches the splendid Mother of
Tomorrow.

The Nations of the Orient

A. Stirling Calder, Frederick Roth, Leo Lentelli, Sculptors

Atop the Arch of the Orient is the superb tableau representing the
types of men that form the Orientals. From left to right - the Arab
Sheik, the Negro Servitor, the Egyptian Warrior, the Arab Falconer,
the Indian Prince and Spirit of the East, the Lama, the Mohammed-
an Warrior, the Negro Servitor, the Mongolian Warrior. On they
come to join the Nations of the West in the great Court of the Uni-

verse. This group is as fine as any group ever seen at an exposition. It rises in its impressive pyramidal height to a climax in the Spirit of the East - a fitting pivot on which to turn the types.

The Alaskan

Frederick Roth, Sculptor

Frederick Roth has fashioned one of the most expressive figures of the Exposition sculpture, but so far above the eye is she and so overshadowed by her companions, that we do not see her in her true light. It is the Alaskan Indian of the Nations of the Occident. She is moving on with her totem poles and blankets. You feel her tug and strain, for her load is growing heavier with each step, and she has yet a long way to go. The modeling of the figure, the foot, the rigid arm and hand, all tell of sustained effort that is truly life-like in expression.

The Lama

Frederick Roth, Sculptor

The priest of Thibet, the Lama, passes on his onward march before you. You do not wonder what race claims him. He is of Mongolian blood. He stolidly passes by, looking neither to the right nor to the left. He is used to being obeyed. His rod of authority tells you that what he says is law. Indifference and arrogance are on his face. His very posture, the very way in which his robe hangs from his shoulders, the position of his nerveless fingers that hold the rod, speak of centuries of indifference to everything except what he thinks.

The Genius of Creation

Daniel Chester French, Sculptor

The Spirit of Creation is a bisexual being, and yet you feel the spirit and not the flesh. Its idealism is of the highest order, being largely produced by the hood drawn far over the face, throwing such deep shadow that personality is lost sight of and only creative force is left. High on a mighty boulder it sits with arms raised. The word has just been spoken and man and woman have come forth - their feet on the serpent, the symbol of wisdom and eternity. At the rear of the group their hands meet as if in mutual dependence, while above appear the Alpha and Omega - "I am the beginning and the end."

The Rising Sun

Adolph Alexander Weinman, Sculptor

This fresh, strong young Sun is about to start on his journey - dawn is soon to break upon the world. With muscles stretched, the wind blowing through his hair, the heavenly joy of the first move expressed upon his face, the vigor of young life pulsating through his body, he will start the chest forward and move those out-stretched wings. Let us preserve this glorious figure for our western city. It would so admirably suggest the new light that has been shed upon San Francisco by the Exposition of nineteen hundred and fifteen, as well as the new light occasioned by the opening of the Panama Canal.

Descending Night

Adolph Alexander Weinman, Sculptor

The figure on the page opposite is a beautiful lyric poem. She might be called "A Hymn to the Night." Every line of her figure is musical, every move suggested, rhythmical. Seen at night, she croons you a slumber song. How subtly Mr. Weinman has told you that she comes to fold the world within her wings - to create thru her desire a "still and pulseless world." The muscles are all lax - the head is drooping, the arms are closing in around the face, the wings are folding, the knees are bending - and she too will soon sink to slumber with the world in her arms. What a fine contrast of feeling between the tense young "Sun" and relaxed "Descending Night."

Winter

Furio Piccirilli, Sculptor

Naked Winter stands before you. It is the period of the year when the leaves are of the trees and the bark is splitting. After the activities of autumn man is resting. The fruits have been gathered - the golden apples and the purple grapes - so man's labors have ceased. It is the period of conception. The sower has just cast forth the seed. Mother Earth will nurture the little seed until the cold winter has passed and the warm sunshine comes again to give each clod its "stir of might."

The Portals of El Dorado

Gertrude Vanderbilt Whitney, Sculptor

There was once among the South American tribes a belief that in a certain far-off country lived a king called El Dorado, the Gilded One. He ruled over a region where gold and precious stones were found in abundance. The story influenced a vast number of adventurers who led expeditions to seek the land of golden treasure; but notwithstanding the fact that their searched most carefully and for long periods, they all failed to find it. The idea of the unattainable gave the suggestion to Mrs. Whitney for her fountain. The gold of El Dorado was used as a symbol of all material advantages which we so strongly desire - wealth, power, fame, et cetera.

Panel of the Fountain of El Dorado

Gertrude Vanderbilt Whitney, Sculptor

In the panel are seen men and women in their mad race for the unattainable. Many have had a glimpse of the Gilded One, and are rushing on to pass the mysterious gate behind which the desires of life await them. Some faint by the roadside or stop in their race for the goal to contend or to loiter by the way, but those nearest the El Dorado increase their speed. Beside the gateway that has only just allowed the Gilded One to pass thru are two mortals who have come close to the land of their desires, but only to find the door shut and slaves beside it barring the way. Their strength is expended, their courage gone in the long race for material things.

Youth

Edith Woodman Burroughs, Sculptor

A little figure of innocence and purity in all her virgin loveliness stands before you - the incarnation of all that is fresh and wholesome. She is only a slip of a girl and yet the dignity of her carriage betokens hopeful days for her womanhood later on. Her form is exquisitely moulded. Those little bony shoulders will all too soon fill out and she will bloom into womanhood. The chief charm of this little lady is her simplicity. Mrs. Burroughs uses such beauty of line, such sweet language to tell her story.

The American Pioneer

Solon Hamilton Borglum, Sculptor

Erect, dignified, reflecting on the things that have been, the American Pioneer appears before us, reminding us that to him should be given the glory for the great achievements that have been made on the American Continent. He it was who blazed the trail that others might follow. He endured the hardships, carved the way across the continent, and made it possible for us of today to advance thru his lead. All hail to the white-headed, noble old pioneer who, with gun and axe, pushed his way thru the wilderness; whose gaze was always upward and onward, and whose courage was unfaltering!

Cortez

Charles Niehaus Sculptor

One of the finest equestrians at the Exposition is Cortez by Charles Niehaus. As we look upon the rider on his sumptuously caparisoned horse we are convinced that he is every inch a conqueror. He is represented absolutely motionless - his feet in the stirrups - and yet you feel that he is a man of tremendous action. You also feel his fine reserve, and yet how spirited he is! This is that intrepid spirit that desired the land of the Montezumas. After determined invasions he conquered the country in the early part of the sixteenth century.

The End of the Trail

By James Earle Fraser, Sculptor

"The trail is lost, the path is hid, and winds that blow from out the ages sweep me on to that chill borderland where Time's spent sands engulf lost peoples and lost trails."

- Marion Manville Pope.

One of the strongest works of the Exposition in its intense pathos is this conception of the end of the Indian race. Over the country the Indian has ridden for many a weary day, following the long trail that leads across a continent. A blizzard is on. He has peered to right and left, but alas! the trail is gone and only despair is his. So has it been with the Indian. His trail is now lost and on the edge of the continent he finds himself almost annihilated.

Panel from the Column of Progress

By Isidore Konti, Sculptor

The four panels on the Column of Progress show the different mental conditions of men on their onward march thru life. In the center of the panel stands the man of inspiration - the eagle, bird of inspiration, perched on his shoulder. He goes thru life with upturned face, depending upon his God for strength. Beside him on the right is seen the warrior who wins his way by sheer physical strength. On his left stands the ascetic philosopher, who through constant vigils "hath a lean and hungry look." To the extreme left falteringly steps the man who fears the unknown future; his wife and mother sustain him by spiritual cheer. The figures are in very high relief so that they seem almost human as you gaze upon them.

The Feast of the Sacrifice

Albert Jaegers, Sculptor

In your imagination you see as of old the harvest procession marching around the fields. It is led by the great bulls for the sacrifice to the gods, that the harvest may yield bounteously. On either side of the bulls are the youths and the maids carrying flowered festoons. The long procession passes on and halts before the altar where the bull being sacrificed, the head with its festoons is placed upon the side of the altar. A most decorative group is this Feast of the Sacrifice - brute strength and the graceful form of the maid making a splendid play of line that most satisfactorily charms the eye.

The Joy of Living

Paul Manship, Sculptor

With perfect abandon come these maidens into the Court of the
Universe, carrying their festoons of wild roses. They bring to the
great festival joy and love of life - a telling addition to all that has
been expressed in the court. They savor of old Greek days, these
maidens of archaic hair and zigzag draperies. Paul Manship loves
the classic which brings with it much of free expression, and he has
adopted the archaic style that recalls the figures such as are seen on
old Greek vases. No one is more joyous among the sculptors than
this man. He has a rarely beautiful gift from the gods.

The Man With the Pick

Ralph Stackpole, Sculptor

An ordinary workman with his pick - and yet how impressed you
are with his sincerity. In him is asserted the dignity, the usefulness,
the nobility of all labor. He helps to turn the wheels of trade, to
further the interests of the world. He works patiently day by day,
notwithstanding the fact that those above him reap the benefits. Mr.
Stackpole has been most happy in his expression. The broad treatment is thoroughly suitable to just such work as this. There are no
accessories employed. The work is absolutely direct.

The Kneeling Figure

Ralph Stackpole, Sculptor

With the love for all that is beautiful in life, in what God has made and in what man has fashioned, the grateful devotee has mounted the steps that lead to the altar at which she offers up her devotion. She bows her head in humble reverence to her God for all that He has given her to enjoy - all that is good, pure, true, beautiful, uplifting. And we onlookers, too, would join the moving throng that bend the knees at the altar of beauty and truth. Across the lagoon we gaze upon the great stillness, and we with her murmur, "Father, I thank Thee."

The Pegasus Panel

Bruno Louis Zimm

There are no reliefs more classically inspiring than are these superb reliefs by Bruno Zimm. The one on the opposite page is of great beauty. The young artist has caught the inspiration of his art - he has bridled Pegasus. Beside him march the Arts - Literature, holding aloft her symbol, the lamp; Sculpture extending in front of her the statuette, a devotee admiring, and Music leading the procession, stilling ever the beasts - a veritable Orpheus. Mr. Zimm has been most successful in the fine working out of his subject in a classical way, for the style of relief work accords well in feeling with the superb classic architecture it decorates.

Primitive Man

Albert Weinert, Sculptor

Long ages past I lived and gave no thought of time or doing aught save going as my fancy took me. Ofttimes I took my bow and arrow and hide me to the mighty forests where herds of Nature's roaming kind served as my food when I required it. Again I followed to the sea where, casting in my net, I drew up myriads of the finny tribe to satisfy my appetite. Oft drew I up such numbers vast that having naught to do but to amuse myself I fed my extra fish the friendly pelican that had become companion in my walks along the shore. A simple man was I with not too many thoughts and only few desires. My body was my foremost daily thought, and little cared I for aught else besides.

Thought

Albert Weinert, Sculptor

The ages have passed on and I more thoughtful have become, for mighty revolutions have gone on within my frame. My mind, a once too puny thing, has year by year grown stronger, until to-day I realize that feeble is my flesh - a thing to be abhorred, and mind does rule above all else. My very face which once was rude and lacked that fire that strong intelligence does give now has a steady purpose and fine spirit writ upon it. It is as if my flesh of old had dropped and like a cast-off cloak had fallen at my feet. Then come those days when tumult as of yore is waged within me, and then I grasp my new-made self and yearn to hold my old position within the body walls. Thought more strong than flesh does wield its strength and back I crouch beneath the feet to stay till Thought is off his guard again.

Victory

Louis Ulrich, Sculptor

Against the blue sky, with wings poised and draperies blown back, appears a Victory from every gable point of the palaces of the Exposition. She is positively charming in her sweep forward. Poised far above you, she holds the laurel wreath ready for the victor. Blessed Victories! We rejoice that there are so many of you for we have found so many victors. Sideview, against the clear blue sky, she suggests the great victory of Samothrace. Mr. Ulrich, we feel sure that the Lady Samothrace has exerted her subtle influence.

The Priestess of Culture

Herbert Adams, Sculptor

There are few sculptors with greater refinement or more cultured reserve than Herbert Adams. He understands the selection of the significant and in many ways seems most fitting to represent the Priestess of Culture. This figure at the base of the dome of the ro-tunda of the Fine Arts Palace, on the inside, is eight times repeated. Simple, dignified, beautifully balanced, with elegance expressed in every line of her garment with its rich border sparingly used, she holds in either arm an overflowing cornucopia, the symbol of what she is able to give you.

The Adventurous Bowman

Herman A. MacNeil, Sculptor

At the top of the Column of Progress where the sea-wind blows thru his locks, stands the Adventurous Bowman, the symbol of achievement. At the base of the column are seen figures representing the progress of men thru life. We watch them file past, but it is with this man of splendid daring, of consummate achievement, that we are most concerned. He has striven and has reached the top. He has only just pulled the chord of his bow, and his arrow has sped on. With confident eye he looks to see it hit the mark. The laurel wreath and palm of victory await his efforts.

Pan

Sherry Fry, Sculptor

You cannot look upon this little figure without feeling that he is inimitably charming. Pan, a god of the woodland, the symbol of the festive side of the Exposition, sits among the shrubs in front of Festival Hall. He has selected a marble capital on which to sit - quick reminder of those classic days when he roamed the Greek glades. Over the cold seat he has spread his fawn-skin. He has just been moving his lips over the pan-pipes, but a rustle among the leaves has caused him to pause in his melody. In the grass he sees a lizard which is as intent on Pan as Pan is on him. Care-free Pan with pointed ear and horned brow, we love thee, for dost thou not give us all our jollity and fun, the tonic for our daily walks!

Air

Robert Ingersoll Aitken, Sculptor

Robert Ingersoll Aitken has added to the cosmical meaning of the Court of the Universe his four elements - monumental, horizontal compositions of pronounced decorative effect. Air is the one of finest poetic feeling. She holds the star to her ear and listens to the music of the spheres. The eagle, the symbol of the air, is used with finely balanced effect. On her back are fastened wings, and man, puny man, is aiming, by attaching wings to himself, to overcome her - a subtle suggestion of airships.

The Signs of the Zodiac

Herman A. MacNeil, Sculptor

One of the loveliest gems of beauty in the Court of the Universe is Herman A. MacNeil's cameo frieze of gliding figures. In the centre, with wings outstretched, is Atlas, mythologically the first astronomer. Passing to left and right glide maidens, two and two, carrying their symbols - for these are the signs of the zodiac. These maids are the Hyades and Pleiades, the fourteen daughters of Atlas. It is as if the figures of some rare old Greek vase had suddenly distributed themselves along the top of the great piers. For absolute refinement, for a certain old Greek spirit in the Court of the Universe, these reliefs could not be excelled.

The Fountain of Ceres

Evelyn Beatrice Longman, Sculptor

The architectural side of the Fountain of Ceres, with its pleasing proportions, is most satisfying to the eye. It was a happy selection to place the Goddess of Agriculture between the Food Products Palace and the Palace of Agriculture. Ceres strikes the keynote of this delightfully beautiful court. With corn sceptre and cereal wreath, Ceres is poised on the globe, the winds of the Golden Gate blowing thru her drapery. Below on the die of the fountain are graceful figures in relief suggesting the decorations of a Greek vase. Eight joyous, happy creatures trip past you, some with tambourines, others with pipes sounding roundelays, or carrying festoons of flowers.

The Survival of the Fittest

Robert Ingersoll Aitken, Sculptor

This is the initial expression of martial spirit, when the first combat is seen and man by physical force seeks to override the power of his fellows. Far back in the childhood of history one finds, as often to-day is the case, that woman is the motive for the fray. Three combatants are here - the one on the right separated from the most powerful by the hand of her who loves him. The cause of the trouble stands at the left, steadfastly watching to see which of those that seek her is to be the victor. A glance tells you that he of powerful build in the center of the panel is to hold sway. He it is who is the most fitting survivor.

Earth

Robert Ingersoll Aitken, Sculptor

A very remarkable figure, her head hanging forward, lies stretched in slumber. It is the sleeping Earth. From her come the great trees whose ramifying roots extend in all directions. Man is seen wresting from her stone and precious metals. Wonderfully has Robert Aitken worked out the Mother Earth idea. She has brought forth many times and yet is ever young. It is keenly interesting to look at "Earth" and then at Michelangelo's "Night" to see the source of inspiration.

Wildflower

Edward Berge, Sculptor

At sight of your form, I seem now to see
A bright stretch of color across a broad lea,
Where the wildflowers sway to and fro in the breeze,
Where the winds sing soft lullabies up in the trees
Where all is as fresh, free and wholesome as you,
Little Wildflower, blooming, so sweet and so true.
And I come from the flight of my far-away dream
As I look and I listen, to me it would seem
That I hear a small voice in a most charming way
Say, "Goodmorrow! Goodmorrow! Take time while you may,
Just step up yet closer; I'll give you a chance
To have something far sweeter than just a bright glance."

Appendix

The Sculptors

The planning, the placing, the naming of all this noble sculpture has practically been done by two men - the late Karl Bitter of New York, a man of great executive and technical ability as well as of immense inspiration, and A. Stirling Calder, on whom the honor for the great bulk of the work rests. Besides acting as personal overseer for the execution of the sculpture of the Palaces and Courts of the Exposition, Mr. Calder has designed the Nations of the Orient, The Nations of the Occident, The Fountain of Energy, The Stars, Column of Progress and its sculpture, and The Oriental Flower Girl. Since the sculpture is one of the strongest factors of this Exposition, we should extend to Mr. Calder our heart-felt appreciation of all that he has done to help make this Exposition such a wonderful, artistic success.

Robert Ingersoll Aitken

Robert Ingersoll Aitken was born in San Francisco in 1878. He was a pupil of Arthur F. Mathews at the Mark Hopkins Institute of Art and later of Douglass Tilden, the well-known California sculptor. He has done a great deal of very strong, compelling work. The examples of his sculpture seen at the Panama-Pacific International Exposition are of pronounced virility and of fine composition. He is a man who excels in technique. He has done in San Francisco the Victory for the Dewey Monument in Union Square, the McKinley Monument, the Bret Harte Monument and the Hall-McAllister Monument. In the Metropolitan Museum of New York is "The

Flame." At the Fine Arts Palace are a number of works from his chisel - The Gates of Silence, the Gates' memorial, being by far the finest.

Herbert Adams

Herbert Adams was born in Vermont in 1858. He has had many advantages, not the least of which were the five years spent in Paris. While there he did the beautiful bust of Adelaide Pond, who afterwards became his wife. In 1890 he returned to America, becoming instructor in the Art School of Pratt Institute, Brooklyn. He has done a number of works for the Congressional Library, the Vanderbilt bronze doors of the St. Bartholomew Church of New York, the tympan of the Madonna and Child in the same church, a statue of William Ellery Channing and many others. His beautiful busts of women are said to be unsurpassed even in France.

Edward Berge

Edward Berge was born at Baltimore, Maryland, in 1874. He was admitted quite early in life to the Maryland Institute of Art, and the Rhinehart School of Sculpture of Baltimore, following this instruction by the usual finishing-off at Paris. He had the good fortune while in Paris to study under the great Rodin. He won bronze medals at both the Pan-American Exposition of 1901 and the St. Louis Exposition of 1904. His many very interesting fountain figures seen at the Panama, Pacific International Exposition have won deserved praise from the many who have seen them.

Solon Borglum

Solon Borglum was born in 1868 at Ogden, Utah. The greater part of his early life was spent on the plains of Nebraska, lassoing wild horses and photographing at the same time every detail of this strange life upon his brain. He spent a short time in California, where he began his life as an artist. Realizing his limitations, he went to the Cincinnati Art School, where he studied some time under Rebisso. It was while here that he spent all of his spare time on the anatomy of the horse. The time soon arrived for a sojourn in Paris. His "Little Horse in the Wind" excited pronounced attention at the Salon that first year abroad and honors were bestowed upon him as long as he remained in Paris. He has given the Indian the greatest attention, and is one of the best sculptors of the red man in the United States. He has but one group in the Fine Arts Palace - "Washington."

Edith Woodman Burroughs

One of the chief women sculptors of the United States is Edith Woodman Burroughs, born at Riverdale-on-the-Hudson, in 1871. She was a pupil at the New York Art Students' League under Augustus Saint-Gaudens, later studying in Paris with Injalbert and Merson. In 1893 she was married to Bryson Burroughs, a New York artist. She has made a specialty of fountain sculpture. No one who has ever seen her Fountain of Youth at the Panama-Pacific International Exposition can forget it. It will always be a source of regret that the appropriation for the Panama-Pacific International Exposition sculpture was reduced, thus preventing the public from seeing the speaking, simple groups of "Arabian Nights Entertainments." Mrs. Burroughs is represented at the Metropolitan Museum of New York by "John La Farge," a remarkably interesting portrait head, full of character. She has the power of speaking her language in a few words - but just the right ones.

A. Stirling Calder

The man at the wheel in the management of all the works of sculpture at the Panama-Pacific International Exposition has been A. Stirling Calder. He was born at Philadelphia in 1870. Having studied four years at the Pennsylvania Academy of Fine Arts, he had the advantage of two years in Paris. For some time he has been connected with the Philadelphia School of Industrial Arts. He is a man of splendid imagination, of dignified and noble purpose, being one of the sincere men of his art who keeps the standards where they should be. One of his early works, "The Man Cub," in the Pennsylvania Academy of Fine Arts, is most original and interesting in its treatment. It stands a most unique figure in the line of sculpture. It is said that his "Martha W. Baldwin Memorial" is one of the best designs for a figure and pedestal yet produced in America. Mr. Calder lived some time in southern California and when there did the sculptured work on the portico of Throop Polytechnic Institute of Pasadena. This work was done by means of enormous castings made in fine concrete. Mr. Calder originated this method and it will probably be the means of revolutionizing the relief work done on many of the public buildings in the future. Mr. Calder's rare intellectual fiber, added to his accurate knowledge of his subjects, with his exalted outlook, has placed him among the foremost American sculptors.

James Earle Fraser

James Earle Fraser was born at Winona, Minnesota, in 1876. His father was a railroad constructor, so that the lad had a good chance in traveling around the country to study the free types and life of the West. Being very impressionable, he imbibed a great deal which he has turned to good account in his chosen work. At fourteen he started to carve figures from the chalk that conventionality required to be used on blackboard problems. At eighteen he entered the Chicago Art Institute, where he stayed for but three months. He soon went to Paris, going first to the Beaux Arts and later to the Colorossi and Julian Academies. He won many honors during his three years stay in Paris. In 1898 he won the prize offered by the American Art Association in Paris for the best work in sculpture. Augustus Saint-Gaudens was on the jury and immediately became interested in the talented boy who later on held the place of chief assistant in the Saint-Gaudens studio. He became instructor of the Art Students' League of New York in 1906, holding the position until 1911. He it was who made the new five-cent piece design - the Indian head on one side, the bison on the other. He is particularly interested in personalities, having done a number of very clever portrait busts. It is enough to look at the portrait bust of Mrs. Harry Payne Whitney's boy to realize what he is able to do in the line of portraiture. He has produced nothing finer in that line. He is a master of character records.

Daniel Chester French

Since the passing of Augustus Saint-Gaudens, Daniel Chester French has been regarded by many as standing at the head of American sculpture. He was born in Exeter, New Hampshire, in 1850. After having one year at the Massachusetts Institute of Technology, he studied with Doctor Rimnier of Boston, the first teacher of art anatomy in the United States. Later he studied with Thomas Ball of Florence, Italy, and a short time in Paris. He has been practically his own instructor. His work is of the noblest type. It is anatomically correct, of a high intellectual order, perfect technique and of fine imagery. His first important work was "The Minute Man" of Concord, Massachusetts. Among his many works are "Death and the Sculptor," "The Alice Freeman Palmer Memorial," the head of "Emerson" (which caused Emerson to say, "This is the head I shave"), "The Milmore Memorial," "The Alma Mater of Columbia College," and finest of all, the wonderful "Mourning Victory" in Sleepy Hollow Cemetery, Concord. His memorials are of high spiritual import.

Sherry E. Fry

Sherry E. Fry was born in Iowa in 1879. He has been most fortunate in having the best instruction, having studied at the Chicago Art Institute, the Julian Academy and the Beaux Arts of Paris, a year in Florence, and later with McMonnies, Barrias, Verlet and Lorado Taft. He has traveled extensively, so has had the opportunity of seeing the best that the world holds for the artist. He won the National Roman Prize in 1908 and held it for three years. He has been a careful student of the Indians. His work at the Panama-Pacific International Exposition is distinctly graceful and decorative.

Albert Jaegers

Albert Jaegers, a man who has taught himself his art, having fine powers of observation and much invention, was born at Elberfeld, Germany, in 1868. He has been an indefatigable worker, holding his art above all else. Solving technical problems by himself, studying the world around him with an intense love in all his undertakings, Albert Jaegers has come to be a power among his fellows. He has exhibited at several Expositions, has done considerable municipal work - the finest figure probably being his "Baron Steuben," of Washington - and many fine portraits. His "Uncle Joe Cannon" in the Fine Arts Palace, shows his power as a portraitist. His work has brought him decorations from the German Emperor.

Isidore Konti

A foreign sculptor living in New York, Isidore Konti has steadily risen in the excellence of his work until to-day he stands among the foremost American sculptors. He was born at Vienna, in 1862. His father's capture by the Viennese in the war against Hungary, where the father lived, and his subsequent compulsory connection with the Viennese army made the son, Isidore, long for the freedom of America. He came to America as a boy, living in Chicago. He exhibited at the Chicago Exposition in 1893, and later attracted much favorable comment at the Pan-American Exposition at Buffalo. His works in the Fine Arts Palace are of a very high order and are exquisitely modeled. The more sober life of the individual, with appreciation of sentiment and longing, are evident in his works.

Leo Lentelli

Leo Lentelli was born in Bologna, Italy, in 1879. He came to the United States in 1903, where he has been permanently located in New York. His most notable work is seen in the Cathedral of Saint John the Divine, New York, where he has done "The Savior with Sixteen Angels" for the reredos. He has recently completed a group which has been placed over the entrance to the new Branch Public Library of San Francisco. He is still another of the sculptors who is self-taught.

Evelyn Beatrice Longman

Evelyn Beatrice Longman has risen constantly in her work since she took her first step in art at the Chicago Art Institute. She was born in Ohio of English parents, being one of six children. At fourteen she began to earn her own living in Chicago, studying at night at the Chicago Institute of Art. She saved her money, using it on her education at Olivet College. She returned to Chicago and studied drawing and anatomy. So clever was she that at the end of the first year she began to teach those subjects at the Institute. Later, she went to New York where she studied with Herman MacNeil and Daniel Chester French. She really made her debut in sculpture at the St. Louis Exposition, where she showed "Victory," a male figure which was so excellent in invention and technique that it was given a place of honor on the top of Festival Hall. In 1907 John Quincy Adams Ward offered a prize for the best portrait bust. This competition was open to all American sculptors. Charles Grafly won in the competition, but Miss Longman won the second place with her "Aenigma." Besides some excellent portraits, she has done two remarkable bronze gates at the entrance to the chapel of the United States Naval Academy at Annapolis, and much fine figure work. Daniel Chester French says "She is the last word in ornament."

Herman A. MacNeil

Herman A. MacNeil was born in 1886, at Chelsea, Massachusetts. After graduating from the State Normal School of Massachusetts, he went to Paris, where he studied under Chapu of the Julian Academy, and two years under Falguiere of the Ecole des Beaux Arts. He came home and soon answered a call to Cornell, where he remained three years. Then three years were spent in teaching art at the Chicago Art Institute. While there, he taught Miss Carol Brooks of Chicago, whom he married in 1895. She is a very clever sculptor herself. Her "Listening to the Fairies," "The First Wave," "The First Lesson," "Betty," in the Fine Arts Palace of the Exposition, readily show how very charming her work is. Mr. and Mrs. MacNeil studied together in Rome for four years and on their return to America established themselves in New York, where the MacNeil studio is. He is the teacher of modeling of the National School of Design, New York. He has made a specialty of Indian subjects, "The Sun Vow," "The Coming of the White Man," and the "Moqui Runner" being some of his best pieces. To him the Indians are as fine as Greek warriors and most worthy of careful study. Whatever he does in sculpture is in its very essence national. He is extremely refined, a superb modeler and one whose every piece of work is strong and of the first rank.

Paul Manship

Standing quite apart from the other sculptors in his special joyous line of work is Paul Manship, a young man from St. Paul, Minnesota, born in 1885. He obtained the Prix de Rome from the American Academy, which prize allowed him to study in Rome and Greece for three years, from 1909 to 1912. His study in Greece gave a most interesting, individual touch to his work, for he united to his fresh, vigorous western style the classic precision of the Greek. He has a certain archaistic mannerism in his work recalling the Aeginetan marbles, which individuality puts a Manship stamp upon his work, striking a distinctly personal note. His statuettes are most charming and natural - little bursts of spirit and intense feeling. His work is always interesting - the kind you cannot pass by. He fills a niche all his own and is a most promising, gifted young sculptor. His "Spring

Awakening" and "Playfulness" in the Twachtman Room of the Fine Arts Palace are delightfully exhilarating little figures.

Charles Niehaus

Charles Niehaus' great talent lies in the lines of monumental sculpture. He was born in Cincinnati, in 1855. He was a pupil of the McMicken School of Art of that city, later attending the Royal Academy of Munich, Germany, where he took the first medal ever won by an American. He has won gold medals at the Pan-American Exposition, the Charleston Exposition and also at the Exposition of St. Louis. His work is of the extremely dignified order, and shows great simplicity of line. It is always the spirit of the work that claims you in all that he undertakes. He has done nothing finer than his "Garfield" at Cincinnati. His Astor Memorial Doors of Trinity Church, New York, his "Doctor Hahnemann" of Washington, D. C., and his "Driller," symbolic of the energy of labor, are among his best works.

Furio Piccirilli

Living in New York in truly Florentine style is the Piccirilli family - a household of five families. It is said that nowhere in America is the old Florentine style of the fourteenth century way of living so well exemplified. The men of the family were marble cutters, but within the last few years Attilio, an elder brother, has been expressing himself in sculpture of a pronounced order. Furio is a young member who is coming to the front thru the very lovely representations of his work at the Panama-Pacific International Exposition. He has given a fine human touch to his work. It stands quite apart in its Italian feeling from the robust American sculpture.

Frederick Roth

Frederick Roth is one of the greatest animal sculptors of the United States and is studying abroad year by year. He was born in Brooklyn, New York, in 1872, and was fortunate in being sent to Berlin and Vienna to pursue his studies when he was very young. He attracted very favorable attention at the Pan-American Exposition by his great originality and technical skill. He is extremely fond of modeling small animals, many of which can be seen in the Fine Arts Palace of the Exposition. "The Equestrienne" is as clever and spirited a small work as he has done.

Ralph Stackpole

Ralph Stackpole, one of the younger sculptors, was born near Grants Pass, Oregon, in 1881. At the age of sixteen he began his art study at the San Francisco School of Design, remaining here for the short period of four months. He later studied with G. F. P. Piazzoni and Arthur Putnam, and considers that from these men he received his best instruction. In 1906 he went to Paris, where he continued his studies at the Ecole des Beaux Arts and Atelier Merces, where he remained two years. He exhibited his work at the Salon in 1901. You meet the man face to face in his work on the Varied Industries Palace. He is sincere, broad, direct. As to his reverence and refined feeling, you need but to look at his "Kneeling Figure" at the altar in front of the Fine Arts Palace to see that he possesses these qualities in abundance.

Louis Ulrich

The world is probably receiving its first introduction to Louis Ulrich, a pupil of the joint school of the National Sculpture Society and the Society of Beaux Arts Architects. He has achieved a "crowning success" in his dignified figure of sweeping lines.

Albert Weinert

Albert Weinert was born at Leipzig, Germany, in 1863. He studied at the Art Academy at Leipzig under Meichior zur Strapen, later coming to America, where he is now located in New York. He has done a great deal of municipal work of a high order, among which can be mentioned sculpture work on the interior of the Congressional Library at Washington, a monument to President McKinley for Toledo, Ohio, a "Lord Baltimore" for Maryland and some very excellent statues on the facade of the Masonic Building, San Francisco. His work in the Court of the Ages has added greatly to the interest of that Court and is forceful, virile work.

Adolph Alexander Weinman

Adolph Alexander Weinman, one of the poets of the sculpture world, was born in Karlsruhe, Germany, in 1870. When but a boy of ten, he came to America with his parents. In his youth he began his student life in art with the great Augustus Saint-Gaudens, attending also Cooper Union, New York. Each year has seen him move successfully ahead until now he is among our finest American sculptors. He is one who stimulates the imagination and raises the standards of art in whatever he models. His work is pregnant with life and is thoroughly individual, so that you feel when you look upon his figures that you have met more than mere bronze or marble. His portraits are of a very high order, many of which can be seen in medal form in the Fine Arts Palace. He lives in New York, where he is well appreciated.

Mrs. Gertrude Vanderbilt Whitney

Mrs. Gertrude Vanderbilt Whitney is one of the foremost American woman sculptors. The Fountain of El Dorado is her first public contribution.

Bruno Zimm

Bruno Zimm, living in New York, was a pupil of the late Karl Bitter. He has designed work for former Expositions, and we trust that his name will be better known in the future. He has added great beauty to the Fine Arts Palace by his classic friezes designed in effective, bold masses. The archaic style used in his work is evident in many of the sculptural forms at this Exposition.

Sculpture Around the Fine Arts Lagoon

The first group of statuary in the following list is located on the south-east side of the Fine Arts Lagoon. Proceeding thence to the left and through the colonnade, the most important subjects will be found in the order described.

Sea Lions. Frederick G. R. Roth
    Most carefully studied as to form and babies; you almost: hear the bark
    of the great mate.

The Scout. Cyrus Edwin Dallin
    The horse and the Indian wait motionless; his hand shading his eyes from
    the sun, the Indian looks intently into the distance for sign of the
    enemy.

Wind and Spray. Anna Coleman Ladd
    A ring of figures - male and female - fleeting and gay - like the wind
    and the spray.

Diana. Haig Patigian
    The goddess of the hunt appears with her bow; the arrow has just left
    the string.

Peace. Sherry Fry
    Quiet, serene, she stands, her brow bedecked with olive leaves; her
    serpent bordered robe may betoken the wisdom of peace.

The Kirkpatrick Fountain (extreme left). Gail Sherman Corbett
    Erected to Dr. Wm. Kirkpatrick, superintendent of Ononda Salt

Springs
    from 1805 to 1806 and from 1810 to 1831, at Syracuse, New York.

The Bison (2). A. Phimister Proctor
    The last of a vanishing race - fine, powerful figures.

Henry Ward Beecher Memorial. J. Q. A. Ward
    A noted American clergyman, lecturer, reformer, author, jour-
nalist;
    lived between 1813 and 1887; a man of forceful personality and
fine
    intellect; he looks the very man of opinions who would not hesi-
tate to
    give them to you - and you would be prone to accept them.

William H. Taft. Robert Ingersoll Aitken
    One of America's greatest statesmen.

Halsey S. Ives. Victor S. Holm
    Was director of the Fine Arts Palace, Pan-American Exposition.

Seated Lincoln. Augustus Saint-Gaudens
    The firm man of thought and action; a replica of the Seated Lin-
coln of
    Lincoln Park, Chicago.

Piping Pan. Louis Saint-Gaudens
    He stands, utterly thoughtless, with his double pipes - passing
the
    hours in amusement; we see him at a musical moment.

Flying Cupid. Janet Scudder
    With the rhyton, the Greek drinking-horn in his hand, Cupid
stands above
    the globe, his little toes holding on firmly so that he will not slip.

A Muse Finding the Head of Orpheus. Edward Berge
    The mourning muse has just chanced upon the severed head of
Orpheus

which had been cast into the stream by the Thracian maidens; short
pieces of marble are left to support parts easily broken.

Michael Angelo. Robert Ingersoll Aitken
We seem to hear him say "And now where next to place the chisel?" He is
creating "Day," which is seen in the Medici Chapel, Church of San
Lorenzo, Florence, Italy.

Nymph. Isidore Konti
A poetic conception of the origin of the stream, from which the fawn
drinks.

Young Pan. Janet Scudder
A favorite subject. Pan is piping his woodland notes and marching to his
own music. Such expressive little hands are those that hold the pipes!
The crab comes up to listen and is held - spellbound.

Wildflower. Edward Berge
Everybody's love! A real darling! A little flower of the fields.

Mother and Child. Furio Piccirilli
A typical mother-expression as she croons over her baby - such a dear
one!

Eurydice. Furio Piccirilli
Orpheus has just looked back-Eurydice, realizing that he is forever lost
to her, looks mournfully after him. Great longing fills her soul.

Boy and Frog. Edward Berge
An independent young chap stands among the rushes - and how expressive

are those toes! The frog, as the fountain, spouts water.

The Dancing Nymph. Olin Warner
    Her pine-cone wand thrown down, her pan-pipes cast aside, the
    ivory-crowned nymph indulges in the dance.

The Outcast. Attilio Piccirilli
    A powerful nude; his very toes portray his grief; surely suggest-
ed by
    Rodin's work.

Boyhood. Charles Cary Rumsey
    The youth who is just beginning to gather his sheaves, looks up
and sees
    the stars! A new treatment in sculpture.

The Pioneer Mother. Charles Grafly
    A simple, dignified woman dressed in home-spun. At her knees
a boy and a
    girl - the future builders of the Western country. She has crossed
the
    cactus-covered plains, has endured the greatest hardships, that
she may
    rear her sturdy little ones to lay the foundations of a mighty
Western
    empire. The bulls' heads are symbolic of sacrifice; oak leaves
symbolize
    strength. She is best seen in the afternoon.

Thomas Jefferson. Karl Bitter
    The seated president, with a world of thought upon his face, has
on his
    lap the Declaration of Independence.

Lincoln. Daniel Chester French
    The rugged man of magnificent understanding, whose every
thought was for
    the betterment of the race.

Relief from the Boston Museum of Fine Arts. Richard H. Recchia
    Illustrating Sculpture.

The Commodore Barry Monument. John J. Boyle.
    A naval hero who died 1803. Fought in the American Revolu-
tion. Victory
    rides at the prow with laurels for him. The "eagle" shows for
whom he
    fought.

Relief from the Boston Museum of Fine Arts. Richard H. Recchia
    This panel represents Architecture.

    Earl Dodge Memorial. Daniel Chester French Earl Dodge, scholar
and athlete, was a greatly beloved Princeton student - a senior who
died just as his college gown was about to be placed upon his
shoulders.

The Young Franklin. Robert Tait McKenzie
    With all his earthly possessions wrapped in a bandana, with
upward gaze
    and confident gait, Benjamin Franklin goes to seek his fortune.

Lafayette. Paul Wayland Bartlett
    The young Lafayette who helped the United States in the Revo-
lutionary
    War and was present at the surrender of Lord Cornwallis.

Relief. Bela L. Pratt
    Representing Sculpture.

Relief from the Boston Museum of Fine Arts
    Representing Sculpture. A relief of simple sweeping lines of
great
    beauty.

The Awakening. Lindsay Morris Sterling
    The day has dawned and with it life awakens.

Beyond. Chester Beach
  A girlish figure wonders what is coming with the future years. Best seen
  from across the road.

William Cullen Bryant (1794-1878)
  An American poet of the first rank. He sits thoughtfully - his
  manuscript before him. Laurels grace his pedestal.

The Sower. Albin Polasek
  Along the field he goes, scattering his seed.

Centaur. Olga Popoff Muller
  This bestial creature is in the act of abducting a beautiful woman. She
  has almost swooned from fright.

The Boy with the Fish. Bela Pratt
  They are singing for joy - the fish seeming to be most comfortably at
  home. Even the little turtle is happy. The little toes must not be
  overlooked.

Returning from the Hunt. John J. Boyle
  The Indian is advancing under the weight of a huge bear across his
  shoulders, and the huge skin of a companion bear being dragged at has
  side.

L'Amour (Love). Evelyn Beatrice Longman
  A group of tender, loving trustfulness. In the background are seen angel
  heads, denoting the spiritual side of love. The serpent below suggests
  the great wisdom born of love. It overcomes all death (the skull). The
  oak leaves symbolize eternal love.

Garden Figure. Edith Woodman Burroughs
    Is this little Adam with the apple, or only a little boy with a ball?

Youth. Victor H. Salvatore
    A little maid in sweet simplicity - against the shrubbery.

Soldier of Marathon. Paul Noquet
    Recalling one of the Niobids of the Uffizi Gallery, Florence. The last
    dying agony of a Greek soldier. His shield stands at the left.

Primitive Man. Olga Popoff Muller
    He hauls the quarry home. Would the nose of primitive man be so lacking
    in primitiveness?

The Scalp. Edward Berge
    The Indian stands exultant! His hands alone betray what has happened.
    The rest of the work is most carefully treated to cover the barbarous
    side of the subject.

Apollo Hunting. Haig Patigian
    "I shot an arrow into the air." This muscular figure recalls the work on
    Machinery Palace done by the same sculptor.

A Faun's Toilet. Attilio Piccirilli
    An awkward, somewhat bashful, wholly boyish faun - his costume an ivy
    crown.

Duck Baby. Edith Barretto Parsons
    A gleeful little soul with chubby toes - more gleeful than the quacking
    ducks she squeezes.

A Maiden of the Roman Campagna. Albin Polasek
    Like an antique bronze from Pompeii. The anemones in her braided hair
    are surely some of those that grow so plentifully on the great Campagna
    beyond Rome.

Head of Lincoln. Adolph Alexander Weinman
    He might have looked like this at the time of his Gettysburg speech.

Daughter of Pan. R. Hinton Perry
    A girlish satyr most intent upon the echoes that she makes when blowing
    through her double pipes.

Mother of the Dead. C. S. Pietro
    The old mother though grief-stricken, accepts the inevitable, while her
    motherless grandson, not understanding, feels that something is wrong.

Destiny. C. Percival Deitsch
    Does Destiny decree that man shall lead, while woman meekly follows, as
    she did in ancient Egyptian days?

Chief Justice Marshall (1755-1835). Herbert Adams
    A dignified seated figure - one of the greatest Chief Justices the
    United States ever had. He held the position from 1801 to 1835. The
    United States is symbolized by the eagle.

Rock and Flower Group. Anna Coleman Ladd
    A decorative group with no special meaning. It might be called "Idle
    Moments."

Great Danes. Anna Vaughan Hyatt
   Watchful Danes guard well the portals. Their names might easily be
   "Keenly Alert" and "In Sober Thought."

Bondage. Carl Augustus Heber
   The mother, tightly bound, thinks not of herself as she turns away, but
   of the weeping child beside her.

Saki - a Sun Dial. Harriet W. Frishmut
   A nymph acts as a pedestal for a sun-dial.

Sun - Dial Boy. Gail Sherman Corbett
   How interested he is in the chameleon which has curiously crept up to
   see who it is that gazes at him.

Sun - God and Python. Anna Coleman Ladd
   Apollo, the god of light, shoots at the python (the symbol of darkness).

Triton Babies. Anna Coleman Ladd
   i.e., Children of the sea-gods, the Tritons.

Bird Fountain. Caroline Evelyn Risque
   The little boy holding the bird clings to the globe with his toes. A
   simple and very appropriate bird fountain.

Prima Mater. Victor S. Holm
   The "first mother" holds her babe to her breast.

   The Fountain of Time, Lorado Taft The great ocean of Time is rolling on, carrying with it men and women of all conditions of thought. Some advance blindly, some hopelessly, some fearfully, some buffeted by the great waves as they roll on.

Nymph - A Garden Figure. Edward T. Quinn
   Showing how any figure gains in beauty by being placed among

the
    shrubbery.

The Dying Lion. Paul Wayland Bartlett
    A powerful and most realistic group. The poor animal is in the
last
    agony - is evidently starving.

New Bedford Whaleman. Beta Pratt
    Such was the type of man who left the town of New Bedford,
    Massachusetts, a whaling port, to seek his occupation in north-
ern water.